Copyright 2010

All rights reserved

Printed in the United States of America

ISBN 1453707662
EAN-13 9781453707661

Tao Te Ching

A new interpretive translation

Written by Lao-tzu

Interpretive Translation by Robert Brookes

Preface

In many ways to try and explain the Tao Te Ching is to admit one's own ignorance of the subject. Which is something I am happy to do, even after spending many years reading it again and again. Although the book seems short it cannot be read properly in an afternoon. Over the years it grows and develops with you, and you soon realize that even though the words remain static on the page they have a life to them which reaches across centuries.

Indeed, this venerable text has been translated countless times, and most booksellers have a shelf with at least half a dozen at any given time. Why does the world need yet another translation?

There are three answers I have for this question. First, the original Chinese text is full of symbols, ideas, and metaphors which make a comprehensive rendering of the text in English impossible. This means that there is a limitless number of equally valid translations that can be created out of it. Secondly, I found that in reading other works I could get a pretty good flavour of a particular translation simply by reading the first verse. And they vary both in quality and the degree of artistic license used in the interpretation (usually the former goes down when the latter is increased). There are some very good translations out there, and the best of them balance making the text accessible to regular readers while maintaining the spirit of the original author. So, I wanted to see if I could do something similar. My own initial experience with the Tao Te Ching was frustrating in that I couldn't seem to find a translation that seemed authentic while being understandable. The third reason for taking on this project was purely selfish, in that I wanted to gain a deeper understanding of the text which could only come from reading and working with it in its literal form. As I continued in the development of the work, I decided that this little book might be of value to others one day, and since you are reading this I hope that it is the case for you.

Acknowledgements

I have to thank all those who have gone before in tackling this work. There have been some excellent translations by other authors and their interpretations of the work have helped to guide my own development.

I also have to thank my friend Michael Canic, who pulled me down this path after introducing him to the literal translation produced by Jonathan Star.

Finally, this work is dedicated with love to my wife, Dr. Kimberly Brookes, who wholeheartedly supports all of these crazy little projects of mine without complaint.

1

The physical path cannot be the eternal way,
just as the spoken word cannot be the eternal truth.

The void manifested the beginning,
the beginning manifested the Tao,
and the Tao is the mother of the ten thousand things.

A mind free from desire
can comprehend the nature of the Tao,
while a mind full of desire
can only witness the Tao's effects.

The Tao and its manifestations originate from the same source.

It is a seemingly incomprehensible mystery
but it is the gateway to one's true being.

2

Beauty is given birth through ugliness
and good is given birth through evil.
Therefore 'is' and 'is not' originate from each other.

Difficult and easy become one another,
long and short form one another,
high and low position one another,
sound and silence define one another,
future and past accompany one another.

Therefore the wise person lives without effort in his daily life.
He practices a wordless doctrine.

Good and bad come to him
and he refuses neither.

He assists in developing people
but he does not presume ownership over them.

He works but is not attached to the fruits of his labour
and does not dwell on his accomplishments.

Because he does not take credit for his accomplishments,
they last forever.

3

By not elevating those with ability
contention would be eliminated.
By not prizing rare objects
thievery would no longer exist.
Shut out the desires of ego and accumulation
and your mind will be settled.

The wise person leads by calming fears and desires,
while filling bellies and strengthening character.

Learning to live simply,
the people are content.
Being content,
they are impervious to deceit.

Act without contrivance,
and everything will be harmonious.

4

The Tao is an empty bowl
inexhaustible to those who use it.

Indeed in its depths lies the origin of all things.

It dulls the sharp edges
resolves perplexities
softens the glare.
Yet it remains a part of the physical world.

This hidden tranquility –
I do not know its origin –
it has existed forever
it will endure forever.

5

Nature does not play favourites,
it regards its creations without sentimentality.
Therefore the wise person also acts in this way.

Nature is like a giant bellows,
empty, yet filled with great potential energy.
The more it moves
the greater its effects.

But too much talk leads nowhere –
it is better to follow the inner path.

The Tao endures forever
it is subtle, profound.
The gateway through which all that is created must pass.

Like reeling silk
unbroken and never ending.
Draw upon it without effort.

7

Eternal heaven
ancient earth.

How can these exist forever?
Because they do not exist for themselves.

The wise person leads by remaining in the background.

Indifferent to ego,
the true self is preserved.
Lacking self-interest,
the true self is realized.

The person of higher virtue is like water,
benefiting the ten thousand things without struggle.
It rests in the lowest places
near the Tao.

Therefore:
In dwelling, choose modest quarters,
in thinking, value stillness,
in dealing with others, be kind,
in choosing words, be sincere,
in leading, be just,
in working, be competent,
in acting, choose the correct timing.

Follow these words
and there will be no error.

A cup too full will soon be spilled,
a sword too sharp will soon be dulled,
too much of anything cannot be kept.

Wealth and power soon turn to arrogance,
and misfortune follows.

Instead, draw back when your work is done.
This is the Tao.

10

Embrace your physical and spiritual natures as one.
Is it even possible to separate them?

When gathering your chi to bring about flexibility,
can you be as supple as a newborn?

When purifying your inner perception,
can you be free of faulty thinking?

When caring for and leading all the people,
can you be without cunning?

As the Tao opens and closes,
can you resist weakening?

With clear awareness penetrating in all directions,
can you remain innocent?

The Tao gives life and cultivates all things
yet it does not claim ownership over them.

The wise person acts but does not take credit.
Leads, but does not rule.

This is a profound virtue.

11

A wheel is useful because it has emptiness at its centre, through which an axle might pass.

A bowl is useful because it is molded around emptiness, waiting to be filled.

A house is useful because of its doors and windows, that allow people to enter and live happily.

Therefore the 'what is' is benefited by the 'what is not'.

Each is served by the other.

Too much brightness blinds the eyes.

Too much sound deafens the ears.

Too much flavour ruins the tongue.

Chasing desires to excess turns your mind towards madness,
and valuing precious things impairs good judgment.

The wise are guided by inner needs,
and are not concerned with the senses.
Therefore the wise person rejects the without,
while embracing the within.

As yang bends toward yin
honour turns into dishonour.
Be wary of becoming bound up in yourself.

What does it mean that honour turns into dishonour?
The need to maintain honour makes one dependent on praise,
so the wise person avoids honour to begin with.

What does it mean to be wary of becoming bound up in yourself?
You become focused on a limited sense of yourself.
But if you are selfless, what misfortune can occur?

Therefore those whose actions accord with the Tao
can be trusted with the greatest responsibility.

14

That which is not seen is called the invisible.

That which is not heard is called the silent.

That which is not felt is called the formless.

Together, these things elude inquiry.

They are confused, and considered to be inseparable:
What is seen is not bright,
what is hidden is not dark.
Stretched to infinity,
it cannot be named.

It returns to nothingness:
shape without shape,
substance without substance.
Illusory, unimaginable.

Encountering it you do not see its beginning.
Following it you do not see its end.

Hold fast to the ancient path of the Tao
in order to master the present.

15

The ancient masters cultivated the mysterious essence.
They were profound, subtle –
beyond our ability to comprehend.
For this reason we cannot know them,
but we can try to describe their existence:

Cautious, as if crossing an icy river in winter.
Vigilant, as if surrounded by unseen dangers.
Reverent, as if receiving honoured guests.

As malleable as ice when it begins to melt,
as unspoiled as an uncarved block,
as receptive as a vast and open valley.

Obscure as muddied water.
But, with stillness, muddy waters clear.
Can you also act while remaining still?

Keeping to the Tao, one does not approach extremes,
one becomes an empty vessel.
It is enough to surrender, without beginning anew.

Reach toward the utmost emptiness,
keep hold of stillness.
Together – the ten thousand things take form.

We recognize that all things return –
now the flowers may be in bloom,
but each will return to the soil from which it sprang.
This returning to the source, in search of stillness,
is the way of nature.

The way of nature is unchanging.
To learn to understand this will provide great insight,
but not knowing this leads to error, resulting in misfortune.

Knowing about the way of nature provides the right perspective,
and the right perspective leads to being just.
Being just leads one to noble behaviour,
noble behaviour leads one towards nature,
and nature is the gateway to the Tao.

Being in accord with the Tao leads to the eternal,
freedom from peril,
until the time comes to return.

The greatest leader is unknown to the people,
a good leader is known and beloved,
an adequate leader is treated with respect,
a poor leader is treated with disdain.

Trust in oneself is not sufficient.
Indeed, the leader is not worthy of such trust from others.

Self-effacing, the leader is careful with words.
Fulfilling duties and accomplishing works for all people,
who then will say that they did it all themselves.

Only when the Tao is forgotten
is there a need for morality and righteousness.

Only when intelligence and cleverness appear
is there a need for pretense.

Only when families are not in harmony
is there a need for filial piety.

Only when the state is in disorder
is there a need for patriotism.

Abandon holiness, discard cleverness
and the people will benefit greatly.

Eliminate philanthropy, put away morality
and the people will regain compassion.

Forsake academic knowledge, relinquish propriety
and the people will lose their anxieties.

Disavow cunning, renounce greed
and there will be no theft.

These lessons are superficial, and could go on forever.
Even then they would still not be sufficient.
One need only rely upon this:

Manifest simplicity, like an undyed silk.
Hold to your natural state, like uncarved wood.
Cast off your ego, and curtail your desires.

20

How great is the difference between approval and disapproval?
How much alike are good and evil?
Must you fear what others fear?
Desolate! This is without end.

Most people desire to be joyful and merry,
as if celebrating at a great feast in the spring.
But the wise person remains placid,
showing no desire,
like an infant who has not yet learned to smile.
And weary, like a homeless wanderer.

Most people desire to possess too much.
But the wise person appears wanting and foolish of mind.

Most people value brilliance and cleverness.
But the wise person seems confused and obtuse,
as if drifting upon windy seas, without direction.

Most people desire to have a useful purpose.
But the wise person appears obstinate, unrefined.

The wise person alone is different from most people,
in that he prefers to draw sustenance only from the Tao.

21

The person of great virtue
has a quality that can come only from the Tao.

The Tao itself is elusive, indistinct.

Indistinct and elusive,
within it is form.
Vague and intangible,
from it comes reality.

Profound and mysterious,
within it is spirit.
This spirit is quite real,
from it comes truth.

Since ancient times, the Tao has never departed.
By means of it, all things are created.
How do I know this is so?
Because it is the nature of the Tao.

22

That which is incomplete will be made complete,
that which is crooked will straighten,
that which is empty will be filled,
that which is worn out will be renewed.

He who has little can only gain,
but gain too much and the way will be lost.

Therefore the wise person holds to the Tao,
and he is the example for all people.

Because he does not show himself, he shines brightly.
Because he is not righteous, he is distinguished.
Because he does not boast, he is successful.
Because he is not proud, he endures.
Because he is not contentious, no one contends with him.

The ancients said:
That which can bend will remain whole.
Is this not true?
To be humble is to remain in the Tao.

To speak few words is the natural way.

The strong wind cannot last the whole morning,
the torrential rain cannot last all day.
It is nature that causes these things,
but even nature cannot cause them to go on forever.
If nature cannot do this, then certainly man cannot do so.

Therefore in whatever you do, let it be done through the Tao.
Follow the Tao and act with virtue.
If you do not follow the Tao, then loss and failure will follow you.

The Tao happily accepts all followers, but so do loss and failure.

Faith in oneself is not enough.
Indeed, the wise person is not worthy of such faith from others.

24

When on tiptoe you cannot stand firm,
when running you cannot go far,
make a display of yourself and you will not be illustrious.
Be righteous and you will not be distinguished,
boast of your abilities and you will not have merit,
be conceited and you will not endure.

People who act in such ways are likely to be detested,
and their path will be burdensome.

However to those who follow the Tao,
these things are like having too much to eat,
and are avoided.

25

Before the birth of all things, there existed an undifferentiated whole.
A solitary void: unchanging, yet operating everywhere,
without exhaustion.
It is therefore considered the source of everything.

I do not know its true name, although some call it Tao.

If compelled to characterize it, I would simply call it great.
For to be great implies that it is far-reaching,
to be far-reaching implies distance,
and to be distant implies returning to the source.

Thus the Tao is great,
Heaven is great,
Earth is great,
the wise person is also great.

In the universe there are four great ones,
and the wise person is one of them.
The wise person follows the laws of Earth,
Earth follows the laws of Heaven,
and Heaven follows the law of Tao.

The Tao, with nothing to follow,
is natural unto itself.

26

Heavy is the origin of lightness,
and tranquility is the ruler of acting rashly.

Therefore when the wise person travels in the world
he never loses sight of his heavy load,
even when he sees magnificent sights.
He dwells in peace, unattached.

How can you be said to be a wise person,
if you behave frivolously in front of everyone?
To be frivolous is to be separated from the source,
just as acting rashly means you have lost control of yourself.

27

The adept traveler leaves no tracks,
the adept speaker reveals no opportunity for reproach,
the adept accountant needs no calculator.

The skilled locksmith opens doors that are locked to others,
the experienced sailor ties knots that others cannot untie.

The wise person is excellent at helping others,
and does not reject any of them.
Indeed, the wise person is excellent at taking care of all things,
and therefore does not reject the physical world.
This is called practicing enlightenment.

The good person is the bad person's teacher,
and the bad person is the good person's lesson.
To honour the teacher you must also cherish the lesson.
Even though this wisdom may seem perplexing,
it is one of the Tao's crucial mysteries.

Know the male, but hold to the female.
Imagine a river flowing through a valley,
never departing from its original path.
Do this and you will return to a state of innocence.

Perceive the bright, but hold to the dark.
Like a river, let yourself flow with virtue,
and set a faultless example for the world.
Do this and you will return to a state of perfection.

Be aware of honour, but hold to humility.
Like a valley, let virtue fill you,
sufficient yet everlasting.
Do this and you will return to the state of the uncarved block.

Just as when the uncarved block is shaped it loses its simplicity,
when the wise person loses his simplicity he is no longer wise.
Therefore it is best to stay on the original path.

Those who attempt to lead by force
will find that this never ends with success.

People are mysterious entities –
try to take hold of them and you will only lose them.
Thus, sometimes it is better to show the way,
and sometimes it is better to follow.

Some people blow hot, while others blow cold;
some people are strong, while others are weak;
some people can overcome adversity, while others give in.

Therefore, the wise person avoids extremes,
withdraws from extravagance,
and discards arrogance.

30

Those who are in accord with the Tao
do not desire to use force when leading the people.
Those who choose to use force on others
can expect others to use force on them.

The good leader achieves his goals,
but stops before going any further.
To go further than necessary is to force success.

Achieve your purpose, but do not be boastful.
Achieve your purpose, but do not show off.
Achieve your purpose, but do not be arrogant.
Achieve your purpose, but do not try to possess it.

When things become overgrown,
they start to decay and will come to an early end.

31

Weapons are never the implements of good fortune,
and they are to be detested.
Therefore, the wise leader avoids them.

Normally the wise leader values patience,
but when at war he values action.
Since he is opposed to the use of weapons,
he uses them only when it is unavoidable,
and even then with great restraint.

To praise victory in war is to rejoice in the slaughter of men.
The slaughter of men causes grief and sorrow to the people,
therefore he who rejoices in this will not be successful.

Fortune follows the restrained,
misfortune follows the ambitious.

Therefore victory in war should not be celebrated,
but instead should be met with mourning.

32

The Tao is nameless and as pure as uncarved wood.
Although the Tao seems insignificant, no one can command it.
The leader that can act in accordance with it
will find that everything is naturally in accord with him.

When heaven and earth in their symmetry combine,
the world is benefited by rainfall.
People will also naturally follow their course in harmony,
without need of regulation.

When people first had regulation,
it became necessary to label things as 'this' or 'that'.
This naming could go on and on,
but it is best to know when to stop.
Knowing when to stop is the basis of avoiding troubles.

To picture the Tao's presence in the world,
think of streams turning into great rivers,
and great rivers turning into seas.

33

Those who know others have wisdom,
but those who know themselves have enlightenment.

Those who conquer others have power,
but those who conquer themselves are powerful.

Be content where you are, and you will always be wealthy.
Act with perseverance and you will meet with success.

Do not lose your centre and you will endure.
He who dies is not forgotten, and in this way lives on.

34

The Tao flows everywhere, in all directions.
All things depend upon it, but it turns nothing away.
It is successful in its purpose, but it does not claim credit;
it nourishes all things, but it does not claim ownership.

Always without desire it is home to even the most insignificant,
and still it is not their ruler.

Therefore the wise person does not act out of the desire
for personal success,
yet he always achieves his goal.

35

Hold to the Tao and all things will follow.
They follow and do not come to harm,
but will enjoy harmony and good good health.

Music and fine food might cause passing strangers to stop,
but the words spoken about the Tao fall flat, they are tasteless –
looking at it is insufficient,
listening to it is insufficient,
but use it, and it is inexhaustible.

If you want something reduced, first let it expand.
If you want something weakened, first let it become strong.
If you want something forgotten, first let it be exalted.
If you want something taken, first let it be valued.

This is a subtle insight:
the flexible overcomes the strong and unyielding.

Therefore, just as a fish should not leave its water,
a country should not show its weapons to the people.

37

The Tao does not act, thus everything is done.
If a leader is in accord with it,
all things will naturally develop.

Afterwards, if old habits arise,
suppress them by remembering the uncarved block of wood.
The natural state of the nameless will truly free people from desire,
and the world will naturally right itself.

38

The person of superior virtue does not practice virtue,
and this is why he has virtue.
The person of inferior virtue cannot forget about virtue,
and that is why he is without it.

The person of virtue does not think to act,
and does not try to control the outcome.
The person of compassion thinks to act,
and also does not try to control the outcome.
The person of righteousness thinks to act,
but tries to control the outcome.
The person of propriety thinks to act,
and if he cannot control the outcome will get involved and force it.

Therefore when the Tao is lost you resort to virtue,
when virtue is lost you resort to compassion,
when compassion is lost you resort to righteousness,
when righteousness is lost you resort to propriety.

Propriety has only a veneer of loyalty and sincerity,
and this is the beginning of discord.
A person who prematurely believes that they comprehend the Tao
sees only its external luster,
and this is the beginning of delusion.

Therefore the wise person prefers substance to the superficial,
dwells in the fruit and avoids the flower,
embraces the within and rejects the without.

39

In ancient times it was natural to be united with the Tao.
Because of this heaven became clear,
earth became tranquil,
spirits became energized,
valleys became full,
the ten thousand things became alive,
leaders ruled the earth with nobility.

What brings this about! Without it:
Heaven would not be clear but would split open,
earth would not be tranquil but would shake,
spirits would not be energized but would wither away,
valleys would not be full but would be exhausted,
the ten thousand things would not be alive but would perish,
leaders would rule with nobility but would be toppled.

Therefore value those rooted in humility,
since the superior person finds his foundation in lowliness.
For this reason leaders refer to themselves as solitary, desolate, hapless.
Is this not because they are rooted in humility?

Thus those who measure their honour have no honour.
Do not shine like jade, instead be humble like a rock.

Turning back is the Tao's motion,
yielding is the Tao's method.

The world and the ten thousand things are born from the 'what is',
and the 'what is' is born from the 'what is not'.

41

When hearing of the teaching of the Tao:
The wise person is diligent about putting it into practice,
the average person can only sometimes follow it,
the inferior person laughs at it –
but if they did not laugh, it not would not be the teaching of the Tao.

There are these established sayings:

The enlightened path appears dark,
and advancing on this path may seem like retreating.
For the path that looks smooth is often rugged.

The greatest virtue appears empty,
and the greatest purity appears tarnished.
The most magnificent virtue seems insufficient,
and firmly established virtue seems frail.
Real virtue is fluid and changeable.

The perfect square has not boundaries.
The greatest talent is slow to mature.
The perfect sound is hard to discern.
The greatest form is without shape.

The Tao remains in the background, nameless.
Yet it is because of this that the Tao is able to nourish and bring success.

42

The Tao produced the one,
the one divided into the two,
the two became the three,
and the three are the source of the ten thousand things.
Each of the ten thousand things carry yin and embrace yang,
their merging produces chi which creates balance.

People feel disdain towards the solitary, desolate, hapless –
yet leaders often refer to themselves by these terms.
Thus sometimes people gain when they are diminished,
and sometimes people suffer when they gain.

What others teach, so do I:
Those who are aggressive and violent never die in peace.
I take this in hand and make it the basis of my teaching.

The softest substances on earth overcome the hardest,
and that which has no form can penetrate the smallest of spaces.

Through this I know that not-acting has its advantage,
and that it is best to teach without words.
Rarely is this practiced or even understood.

44

Your name or your health – which is closer to you?
Your health or your possessions – which is worth more?
To gain or to lose – which is more harmful?

Those with excessive desires incur great cost.
Those who guard wealth surely suffer great loss.

To avoid disappointment, know what is sufficient.
To avoid trouble, know when to stop.
If you are able to do this, you will last a long time.

45

The most perfect thing can seem flawed,
but this does not impair its usefulness.
The greatest abundance can seem inadequate,
but this does not limit its utility.

The greatest truth appears wrong,
the greatest intelligence appears stupid,
the greatest gain appears to be a loss.

Activity overcomes the feeling of being cold,
and keeping still conquers the feeling of being hot.
Peaceful tranquility – this is the right way in the world.

When the Tao prevails in the world,
fast horses do slow work in the field.
When the world is without Tao,
horses are bred for war.

There is no greater misfortune than not knowing what is enough.
There is no greater fault than the desire to possess.

Therefore, if you are satisfied that what you have is enough,
you will always be content!

47

You do not need to step out of your door
to understand the ways of the world.
You do not even need to look out of your window
to perceive the way of the Tao.

The greater the distance you travel,
the greater your understanding is diminished.

Therefore, the wise person:
does not need to go out and yet he knows,
does not need to see and yet he understands,
does not strive and yet he succeeds.

He who pursues knowledge desires to accumulate more each day.

He who pursues the Tao desires to diminish more each day.
He continues to decrease until attaining the realization of non-action –
not acting, but leaving nothing undone.

Thus you lead by not interfering,
since striving to lead will never be enough.

The wise person is without a decided mind,
thus his actions are based on the minds of the people.

The wise person treats the good person with goodness,
he also treats the bad person with goodness –
this is how you become good.

The wise person gives the truthful person his trust,
he also gives the untruthful his trust –
this is how you become trustworthy.

The wise person lives in the world with
united and harmonious activity,
his heart and mind mixing with the people as water mixes in the ocean,
seeing all people as his innocent children.

50

You originate in life, but always return to death.

Three in ten people focus too much on extending life.
Three in ten people focus too much on fearing death.
Three in ten people focus on living life to the fullest
and thus find an early death. Why is this so?
Because such people live to excess.

It is said of the one in ten who successfully preserve their life:
When traveling they do not fear the wild buffalo or the tiger.
When in the battlefield they avoid armour and weapons.

The wild buffalo can find no place to pitch its horns,
the tiger can find no place to to sink its claws,
the soldier can find no place to thrust his sword.

Why is this so?
Because he has no place for death in his life.

51

The Tao gives life to all things,
then the Te* nourishes them.
The Tao and the Te form all things in this world,
and then the environment matures them.

Therefore all things in this world honour Tao and treasure Te.
This happens without any demand, it happens naturally.

The Tao gives life to them and the Te nourishes them.
The Te grows them and develops them,
protects them and prepares them,
supports them and shelters them.

The Tao gives birth but does not take possession of them.
The Te helps them but does not require gratitude,
it develops them but does not subordinate them.

This is the root of the mysterious Te.

*Te: Virtue, or the Tao in action. Te is normally translated as 'virtue' through the book.

52

The world was given a beginning
by that which could be called the world's mother.
To know the mother is to know the son,
and in understanding the son you in turn keep close to the mother.
Until the end, you will be free from danger.

Block your senses, close the gates of desire,
and throughout your life you will have no trouble.

Open your mouth, meddle in the affairs of others,
and to the end there will be no saving you.

Perceiving the insignificant is called enlightenment,
abiding to the yielding is called strength,
employing brightness restores your insight,
without surrendering your life to misfortune.

This is called cultivating the eternal Tao.

53

If I possessed the smallest amount of sense,
I would follow the path of the Tao.
For this reason I fear to stray.

The path of the Tao is very straight,
yet others prefer to be sidetracked.

When the palaces are full of excessive splendor,
the fields are full of weeds and the granaries are empty.

To dress in elegant clothing, carrying fine weapons,
gorging in food with wealth and possessions in abundance –
this is called boasting of thievery.

Indeed, this is not the way of the Tao.

54

One who is well planted in the Tao cannot be uprooted,
one who has a firm grasp of the Tao will not let it slip away.
Your descendants will not cease in their honour of you.

Cultivate the Tao in your person and virtue becomes genuine,
cultivate the Tao in your family and virtue will overflow,
cultivate the Tao in your community and virtue will be lasting,
cultivate the Tao in your nation and virtue will be in abundance,
cultivate the Tao throughout the world and virtue will be pervasive.

Thus the person must be considered as a person,
the family must be considered as a family,
the community must be considered as a community,
the nation must be considered as a nation,
the world must be considered as a world.

How do I know this is so?
By means of the cultivation of virtue.

55

One who possesses virtue in its fullness resembles a newborn child.

Poisonous insects will not sting him,
fierce animals will not attack him,
predatory birds will not seize him.

His bones are weak, his muscles are soft,
yet his grasp is strong.
He has not yet experienced the union of man and woman,
yet his genitalia will be erect.
Indeed, his life force is at its peak!
All day he cries but does not become hoarse.
Indeed, his inner harmony is at its height!

To have inner harmony is to be in accord with the eternal,
and to be in accord with the eternal is to be enlightened.

To force the growth of your vitality is ill fated.
To direct the life force with the mind will make you strong,
but creatures that are strong in this way soon are exhausted.
This is not in accord with the Tao,
and that which is not in accord with the Tao soon comes to an end.

Those who understand the way do not talk about it,
and those who talk about the way do not understand it.

Therefore the wise person:
Closes his mouth,
locks his gates,
tempers his sharpness,
simplifies his problems,
softens his glare.

Unite yourself with the low –
this is the profound harmony.

Where there is no attachment,
there is liberation from aversion.
Where there is no profit,
there is liberation from loss.
Where there is no honour,
there is liberation from disgrace.

Therefore this is the most cherished way on earth.

57

Use justice when leading the people,
employ cunning when conducting a war.
But it is through non-action that the world is won over.

How do I know this is so?
Where there are more restrictions and prohibitions,
there is also more poverty.
Where there are many sharp weapons,
there is also more chaos.
Where the people are full of clever schemes,
there are also strange outcomes.
Where there are many laws and edicts,
there is also an abundance of criminals.

Therefore, the wise person:
Practices non-action so that the people are naturally transformed.
Welcomes quietude so that the people will naturally be civilized.
Does not interfere so that the people will naturally be prosperous.
Avoids desires so that the people will naturally choose to live simply.

When the government is unobtrusive,
the people live simply.
When the government is interfering,
the people are contentious.

Misfortune is the place that happiness calls home,
just as happiness is the hiding place for misfortune.

Can you perceive when your limit is reached?
Is there not one correct way?

The just will return to the perverse.
The good will return to the sinister.
The people will be lead astray for a long time.

Therefore the wise person is sharp and yet does not injure,
is pointed but does not penetrate,
is true to the path but does not bully,
is bright but does not blind.

In leading the people or attending to nature,
there is nothing better than moderation.

Only through practicing moderation can you quickly yield.
To quickly yield depends upon your abundance of virtue,
your abundance of virtue means nothing cannot be overcome,
nothing that cannot be overcome means you know no limits,
knowing no limits, you can thereby lead the state.
To lead the state, be its mother, and you will last a long time.

This is called having deep roots, a solid trunk.
Long life, enduring insight.
It is the path.

Leading a great state is like frying a small fish.

When the leader of the state is in accord with the Tao,
the deceitful will lose their power.
It is not that they lose their power,
but that their power does not harm the people.
It is not that their power does not harm the people,
but that the wise person who governs does not harm the people.

Neither cause harm,
therefore virtue is unified and returns to both.

A great state should flow down-river,
so that it will become the world's meeting ground.

The weak who are tranquil will outdo the strong,
it is through stillness that one is able to yield.
When the strong yields to the weak,
the strong wins over the weak.
Therefore the weak, being low, wins over the strong.

Sometimes you must yield in order to win,
and sometimes maintaining a low place leads you to win.

The large state stays within its boundaries,
and wants only to care for its people.
The small state stays within its boundaries,
and wants only to serve its people.

Both are able to obtain what they want,
when the strong yields to the weak.

The Tao is the source of the way things flow.
The good person treasures it, the bad person is protected by it.
Pleasing words can thus find a market,
honourable actions can thus raise a person up.

Why then forsake those who have no goodness?

The emperor selects his three ministers,
each preceded by horses and presenting jade disks.
But would it not be better to offer this simple teaching?
This is the reason why the ancients treasured the Tao.

Did they not say that even criminals who have sought to obtain it are thereby freed?

For this reason, the Tao is the treasure of the world.

Act without doing.
Work without being busy.
Savour without tasting.
Make great the small and make many the few.
Reward malice with kindness.

Plan for difficulty when it is still easy.
Achieve the great by attending to the small.

All great difficulties in the world, in the beginning,
were easy to solve.
All great achievements in the world, in the beginning,
seemed inconsequential.

Therefore the wise person never strives for the great,
although he accomplishes greatness.

Truly, one who takes commitments lightly rarely keeps his word.
When a person takes things lightly there will surely be great difficulty.

Therefore the wise person confronts difficulties with seriousness,
and in the end is without problems.

That which is at rest is easily held.
That which has not yet emerged is easily prevented.
That which is fragile is easily shattered.
That which is small is easily dispersed.

Deal with things before they emerge,
set things in order before there is discord.

The giant tree starts out as the tiniest shoot,
the tallest tower starts out as a single brick,
the longest journey starts with the first step.

Taking action leads to failure,
seizing at things results in their loss.
Therefore the wise person does not act and does not fail,
he does not grasp and thus loses nothing.

People pursue their affairs, constantly near success,
and yet ultimately meet with failure.
If you are as careful at the end as at the beginning,
your activities will not end in failure.

The wise person seeks freedom from desire
and does not treasure precious things.
He learns not to hold onto ideas.

He restores what others pass by,
and thereby assists in their development naturally.
He does not presume to interfere.

In ancient times those who practiced the Way
did not seek to enlighten others, they kept it hidden.

People are hard to lead because of their cleverness.
Therefore those who use cleverness to lead do so to their detriment.
However leading without cleverness brings good fortune.

To recognize these two principles is to know a natural pattern.
To know this natural pattern is to understand a profound virtue.
This profound virtue is deep and far reaching!

All things return to the source,
thus obtaining complete harmony.

The reason why a great river can be the king of a hundred valleys
is because it is good at staying in the lower position.

Therefore:
Wanting to rule the people,
you must place yourself in a humble position.
Wanting to lead the people,
you must place yourself behind.

The wise person is able to dwell above, and not weigh down the people.
The wise person is able to stand in front, and not obstruct the people.

Therefore the world is glad to support him and does not tire of it.
Because he does not contend, the world is not able to resist him.

The world calls my teaching great, and like nothing else.
Because it is great it seems useless.
If it seemed useful, how long ago would it have disappeared!

I have three treasures, guard and preserve them:
The first is compassion.
The second is moderation.
The third is humility.

The compassionate have the power to be brave,
the frugal can afford to be generous.
One who does not dare to be first can therefore succeed and endure.

If you renounce compassion but try to be brave;
if you forsake frugality but try to be generous;
if you discard humility but try to lead –
things are sure to end in failure.

Mercy in battle brings victory.
Compassion in defence brings invulnerability.
As this is in accord with nature, nature is the protector.

The skillful soldier is not violent,
the skillful fighter is not angry,
the skillful conqueror is not vengeful.
The skillful leader puts himself below others.

This is called the virtue of non-contending,
the means of employing the abilities of others.
It is known as being in accord with nature's highest principles.

Experts in strategy have a saying:
I dare not attack first but instead take the defence.
I dare not advance an inch but instead retreat a foot.

This is called advancing without moving forward,
grasping without showing one's arms,
confronting without attacking,
taking up weapons with no soldiers.

The greatest misfortune comes from underestimating the opponent.
Make light of your opponent and you risk losing everything of value.

When evenly matched opponents meet in battle,
the one that yields is the one that wins.

My teachings are easy to understand,
and easy to put into practice.
However the people do not understand them,
and do not put them into practice.

My teachings have an ancient source,
but the people are ruled by the affairs of the day.

Just as the people do not understand my teachings,
they do not understand me.
Those who understand them are rare.
Those who follow the path are distinguished.

Therefore the wise person clothes himself in rags
to hide the jewel he carries within.

To know without thinking you know is best,
to not know but think you know leads to disaster.

Truly, naming a condition as a disease
is why you cannot be free of disease.

The wise person is free of disease,
since he recognizes the disease of having disease,
and therefore he is healthy.

When the people do not fear consequences for their actions,
then great disaster follows.

Do not interfere with their homes,
and do not harass their livelihoods.

When the people are not oppressed they do not grow weary.

Therefore the wise person knows himself but does not parade himself,
he takes care of himself but does not exalt himself.
He rejects the without,
while embracing the within.

Courageousness taken to fearlessness leads to death.
Courageousness not taken to fearlessness leads to survival.
Of these two things, one brings benefit, the other brings harm.

Who knows why nature rejects some and not others?
Even the wise person is unsure of this.

The Tao does not contend,
yet it is victorious.

It does not speak,
yet it gives answers.

It does not ask for anything,
yet it is naturally provided for.

It appears to be slow,
yet its plans are always realized.

Its net is vast and wide,
and nothing passes through.

74

If the people do not fear death,
how can the threat of death frighten them?

Suppose that the people do fear death.
Would a person break the law,
knowing that he would be arrested and put to death?
Would he put himself in that position?

There is one executioner.
If a person were to take his place,
it would be like taking the place of a master wood carver.
There are few that would not injure themselves.

75

Why do the people starve?
It is because those at the top eat too much, and taxes are too high.
This is why the people starve.

Why are the people difficult to lead?
It is because those in authority are meddlesome in their affairs.
This is why the people are difficult to lead.

Why are the people frivolous with their lives?
It is because they are striving for a life that is too full.
This is why the people are frivolous with their lives.

Truly, only one who does not live only to fill their life,
is one who properly values life.

A person at birth is yielding and weak,
but at death they are stiff and unyielding.
The grass and trees when growing are tender and delicate,
but when dying are brittle and dry.

The stiff and unyielding are the companions of death,
while the yielding and tender are the companions of life.

Therefore we see that unbending armies cannot conquer,
and the strongest tree feels the axe.

The mighty will fall down low,
but the humble will rise up.

The way of the Tao can be compared to stretching a bow.
When the string is high it is pulled down,
when the string is low it is raised up.

In this way excesses are diminished,
and inadequacies restored.
The Tao takes from abundance
to balance scarcity.

The way of people is different.
It takes from where there is already not enough
to further provide for those with too much.

Who can have abundance and still offer it to the world?
Only the wise person, the person of Tao.

Therefore he acts but does not exact gratitude.
He accomplishes but does not claim credit.
Why? Because he does not hold his virtue up for display.

In this world there is nothing more yielding than water,
yet attack it with strength and you cannot conquer it.
In all the world, there is no substitute.

The flexible surpasses the inflexible,
the soft overcomes the hard.
There is no one that does not know this,
but there are few who can put it into practice.

Therefore the wise person says:
He who can suffer his nation's faults
is to be known as its leader.
He who can bear his nation's disasters
deserves to be leader of the world.

Do these words seem paradoxical?

Making peace between great enemies –
surely there will be lingering hatred?
What can remedy this?

The wise person holds to the lower position,
and does not make claim on others.

He who possesses virtue keeps his promises.
He does does not possess virtue insists on payment.

Even though the Tao is without preference,
it is in accord with the virtuous person.

It is better to have a small state with few people,
even if they possess a thousand-fold more tools than needed,
and do not use them.

Let them value their lives,
and have no desire to move away.
Even if they have boats and carriages,
they will have no place to go in them.
Even if they own weapons,
there will be no occasion to display them.

Let them return to using knotted ropes for counting.
Delight in their food.
Be pleased with their clothes and content in their homes.
Find joy in everyday life.

Neighbouring communities in sight of one another –
so close that the roosters and dogs can hear each other.
The people grow old and die,
never having even visited one another.

Sincere words are not pleasing,
pleasing words are not sincere.

Quarrelsome people are not good,
good people are not quarrelsome.

The wise person is not erudite,
the erudite person is not wise.

The wise person does not accumulate for himself,
since his gain comes from giving to others.
Thereby devoting himself to others,
he becomes richer and richer.

The Tao may be sharp, but it does not injure.

The way of the wise person is the Tao.
He accomplishes much, but does not strive or contend.

About the Translator

Robert Brookes has been studying the Tao Te Ching and Asian philosophy for 15 years, with primary interests in Taoism, Buddhism, Tai Chi Chuan, Qigong, and mindfulness meditation. He holds a B.A. in Sociology from Wilfrid Laurier University and an M.B.A. from Edinburgh Business School. He resides in a small town in Southwestern Ontario, Canada.

To contact the translator of this work, please email:
rbrookesTTC@gmail.com

Made in the USA
Lexington, KY
07 April 2015